Dedication

This book is first dedicated to my Lord and Savior, Jesus Christ without Whom it would not have been possible. Then to my children who have always been the driving force in my life, I say that I love you all. To my husband, Christopher, who has always supported me in all my endeavors. To my parents, John Arthur, and Beatrice Dingle, they showed me love and support and never let me down. To my other parents, Christopher, and Rosa Greene, I thank God because they took me in as their very own. I would also like to dedicate this to all the mothers and fathers that know the struggles of dealing with rearing up children, who know the heartaches of having to deal with the never-ending issues while partaking in the joys of your lives. I pray that this book educates and brings enlightenment.

WORLD OVERCOMERS:

Helping Your Teens Survive in Today's Society When the World Says It's Okay

WORLD OVERCOMERS: Helping Your Teen Survive in Today's Society When the World Says It's Ok.

Table of Contents

INTRODUCTION

World Overcomers is a self-help book written with Biblical principles to help parents deal with topics and issues that our children are confronted with today. It is based on God's teachings. It will help you to broach conversations that will otherwise be difficult to deal with.

1 John 4:4, KJV:

- "Ye are of God, little children, and have overcome them: because greater is He that is in you than he that is in the world."
  God tells us that when we are in Christ, we are world overcomers.

This is the attitude that we as His children must take on. We must know with all our hearts that the devil has no power over us. We have dominion in Christ Jesus.

World Overcomers will help you to follow God's Word and to lead your children so that they will be overcomers in Christ. It is my solemn prayer that everyone who reads this will be empowered and gain

a deeper understanding on how to deal with the topics

that are discussed herein.

With the ever-growing trends of peer pressure, it

is becoming increasingly more difficult to keep your

teens and sometimes tweens, away from the ways of

the world.

Premarital sex, drinking, and drugs are becoming

a norm today. Not doing drug's is frowned upon. The

non-social drinker is an outcast. Then God forbid if

they are virgins. They are treated like lepers. Girls are

pressured into sex with the ever-popular one-liner: "If

you love me, you will do it." Boys are made to feel like

they are gay if they are not doing it. A large amount

are coaxed into sex by being told that everyone else

is doing it.

There are some that have made pregnancy pacts

as well as suicide pacts. They are made to feel like

freaks if they are not following the crowd. We as parents must instruct our children, daughters, and sons, that it is all right to stand out from the crowd instead of mixing in with it.

The attacks on our children have increased because the agenda of the enemy is to take them out before they can fulfill their purpose in God. The ways of this world contradict the ways of God. The world says that there is nothing wrong with a man and woman living together before marriage. God calls that fornication, and it is a sin. The says that it is acceptable for men to marry men and women to marry women. God says in, [1] Cor. 6:9 that men should not be abusers of themselves with mankind. Now that does not say that He will not forgive you for your sins, but the Word of God tells us that we must first repent, turn from our wicked ways, seek His face, and ask for forgiveness. Then He will forgive and deliver you, but you must want deliverance.

Like everything else with God, your deliverance is there for you to accept or to reject. God's love is the only thing that you do not have to choose whether you accept it or not. His love is unconditional. We do not have to do anything to receive it, but we do have to build a relationship with Him. Here are some things that we must do to build a relationship: be it with God, our children, or others.

Unit 1

Building Relationships by Opening the Lines of Communication

In order to build a house, you must begin with the foundation. Have you ever seen a house being built from the roof down? I am going to guess that your answer is a resounding: "NO!" Therefore, there is an order to building relationships. So, with our children, as with anyone else, we must build relationships, and in order to do that, we must begin with a solid foundation. That foundation is communication.

Communication is the key to opening doors that the enemy will try to keep closed. He will try to close these doors by building walls that will shut down all communication, thus, stifling solid relationships. Relationships that will help to strengthen and build our children. They will help to keep them close to us and bridge the age-old gap that separated adults and children for all time.

When our babies were born, we found it hard to communicate with them because we did not understand them. As time passes, we develop a relationship that allows us to understand when our baby cries, why she/he is crying, what they want, and if they are hurting. We can tell if the cry is because he/she is hungry, sick, wet, or just want to be held. It allows us to communicate, with our baby and that helps us to know just what they need and when they need it.

As our children grow, the roles reverse. As babies, we had to develop a relationship with them to be able to communicate. As they get older, we must communicate with them to keep those relationships. The older they get, the closer we must draw them to us. We must be understanding without getting into a friendship role. We must know the difference in the role of a parent and a friend. So, communication is key.

Lack of communication brings about a breakdown of relationships. Our children may feel misunderstood, unwanted, mistrusted, misused, abused, and most importantly, unloved. These can and have led to the ever-increasing suicide rate in this country today among our teenagers. If you do not verbally express your love and affection for your child or show it with your actions, they will not believe that you love them. This may also cause them to seek that love from other sources. That source can come in the form of an abuser: both physically and emotionally. It can come in the form of someone who is very controlling. It can even cause them to grow up and not know how to parent their own children. So, we see that being loving and nurturing parents is pertinent.

Parents be aware. Do not make the mistake of thinking that you can show your children love by buying them things. Things cannot show love, nor can they parent your child. We, as parents, sometimes make the mistake of giving our children everything they want because we did not have it when we were children, and we overcompensate with our own children. Now, do not get me wrong. There is nothing wrong with providing everything that your child needs. Our Father in Heaven does the same for us. The problem comes in giving a child everything she/he wants. This gives many children a sense of 'entitlement.' They can begin to believe that the world owes them something. Then when things do not go their way, they cannot handle it and it can lead to cases like the [2]Menendez brothers, for example. With all they had and with all that their parents gave them, they felt it was not enough and are now spending time in prison for murdering them on August 20, 1989 and were sentenced for their murders in 1996.

Communicating with your children may be hard but it is a necessity. We as adults sometimes do not realize it but children have pressures in life as well. They have things that stress them out on a day-to-day basis. They need to be able to vent on occasion without being judged or punished. I know I wished I could have gone to my parents about a lot of the things that I was going through. Who knows, maybe I could have. I just did not feel that I could.

During the time I was coming up, there were certain things that you simply did not or could not talk to your parents about. I am quite sure that my own children wished that they could have come to me, and I find myself wishing that they had come to me. The world we live in today is different. It is imperative as a parent that you discuss such matters as sex, drugs, drinking, and suicide issues (among others) with your children.

Opening the Lines can be difficult, but you must find a way to do it. Find out what your child's likes, or dislikes are. Find out what her hobbies are. Spend time with her/him and get to know them better. The best way to get to know someone is to spend time with that person. Quality time. Know who they are surrounding themselves with. Know the people in their inner circle. The greatest influences in our children's lives are those from the outside. We must turn the tables on this to ensure that we are their greatest influences. This comes with communication.

To prove the importance of communication, think about when you got with your significant other. You knew absolutely nothing about them or little to nothing about them. The more time you spent with them, and the more you communicated with them, you began to learn many things about them. Things that helped the relationship to grow. Things that caused you to open your heart and let them in. It is the same way with your child. Some parents have the misconception that just because it is their child, they know them. Not true. They can be in the same house with you for 20 years and you do not know what you should know about them: what their dreams or aspirations were, are far from you because you have not set the foundation by opening the lines of communication. You may know the surface things, but the deeper things are far from you.

Begin opening the lines a little at a time. If you do not already have a relationship   with your child where they open up to you about things, this will be difficult at best for them. You must make this transition into this new relationship as easy as possible for them. Try taking them out to dinner and giving them a chance to talk about their day or choose something that they enjoy doing. During this time together, make them feel comfortable enough to open up to you. You may even try opening up to them about something that happened to you that you wished that you could have talked to your parents about. Be sure that it is not something that will traumatize the child the first time out. Ask God for a good icebreaker. Ask Him to give you the right words to make you, as well as your child, feel comfortable. Ask Him for the wisdom on how to manage the situation.

You may have to go out to several dinners before you build up a rapport with your child where they feel comfortable enough to open up. Once that happens, I would suggest that you devote more time to him/her. Take them on a weekend excursion so that they will be free to open up and let you in on all of his/her feelings. Do not rush it.

There are no time limits. Your child's well-being is at stake. The enemy is trying to destroy them by destroying their young minds.

Now that you have built the foundation by opening the lines of communication, it is important for you to listen to them. Be prepared for what you might hear. Do not judge or condemn. Be rational. It may be hard, but you must do it if you want your child to trust you. It is also imperative that you speak with them about topics that are controversial today. It is better to hear the truth coming from you than from a friend that knows as little as they do. Show them that they can trust you. Again, do not cross the line from being a parent to a friend. There is enough time for that once the boundaries have been set. That is after they have become adults and they know what lines not to cross. Now that the foundation is set, start with the topics that are the most pressing at the time. Those things that can alter your child's life: spiritually, physically, and emotionally.

Remember, it is not always easy building relationships. Especially with someone that you have not taken the time to do so. Our children are no different. They are just young people on their way to adulthood and they must be shaped and taught in a way that they will be able to handle relationships with you, their parents; their siblings; school mates; and eventually, their own mate.

Communication and building relationships go hand in hand to shape who your children will be later in life. It will help to develop their minds as you create an atmosphere of love, caring, nurturing, understanding and patience. Yes, I said patience. It is an important part of being the kind of parent that you need to be and your child needs you to be. Having patience is not always an easy thing to have, but even the Word of God tells us how important it is. (1) It says that patience is a virtue. (2) Patience brings peace. (3) Patience is better than pride. (4) Patience helps us go through trials with a hope that it will soon end.

Having patience lets God know that we trust Him to fix the situations in our lives. It tells Him that we know beyond a shadow of a doubt that this too shall pass. When we worry about things instead of giving them to God and waiting patiently for Him to come through for us, it causes stress, and we all know that stress is a silent killer. So, go to God with all our cares and problems and He will take care of them.

Sometimes we as parents think that just because our children are young, they do not have stress in their lives. Stress has no age limits. No matter how young we are or how old we are, there are things in our lives that can stress us out. The enemy will bring situations into our lives that will cause us to stress out if we do not know how to go to God and seek His guidance and His help. Therefore, communicating the fact that a relationship with God is a vital and important one to have to our children should be foremost as we build lasting relationships with them.

Building relationships with our children will avoid those things in their lives that will cause them to become rebellious and ill-mannered. Do not get me wrong, even when you have done your level best to communicate with your children or to teach them the way that their life should go, it is still possible that they will go astray. That does not mean that you are a bad parent, it simply means that children develop their own characteristics and attitudes. They will have to find their own way as they navigate through the choppy waters of life. But rest assured if you have taught them properly, they may stray from it, but they will not depart from it.

NOTES ON COMMUNICATION

_____
_____
_____
_____
_____
_____
_____
_____
_____
_____
_____
_____
_____
_____
_____
_____
_____
_____
_____
_____
_____
_____
_____

Unit 2

Premarital Sex and Your Teen or Tween

Talking about sex with your child can be one of the hardest things to do for some parents. They would rather have a tooth pulled without anesthesia (I still would), but it is in the best interest of your child that it be done. Not only because teen pregnancy in this country is a problem, but HIV/AIDS and other sexually transmitted diseases are as well. So, our children's lives are on the line if they are not properly educated. I am sure that you, as the parent, would rather that education come from you.

There are many Biblical principles against premarital sex. We know that it is wrong but truthfully, we also know that it is happening and that no matter how much we talk, we cannot stop a determined teen. Think about it, we were teens once. Were our parents able to stop us? These Biblical principles may be the best way to help deter your child from taking on adult actions with a child's mind. I will be discussing a few of these to help guide you through this challenging task of what is called the 'sex talk.'

The first thing that you must know is that your child is not going to want to discuss this with you. It can be embarrassing for them. But it is your job as the parent to make her feel comfortable enough to listen. That is why you took the time to build the foundation.

Make her feel comfortable by letting her know that it is not easy for you either but because you love her, it is necessary, and you are willing to do whatever it takes to ensure her safety.

Sex is a natural part of life, but it should be done at the proper time. It should be saved until marriage. Premarital sex goes against the commands of God.

We, as parents, must be sure that our children understand just how important saving themselves for marriage is. There are (3) basic reasons why waiting for marriage is not only being obedient to God's Word as it states in 1 Thessalonians 4:3-4 but it is also good for the couple.

1) You and your spouse will share something that no one else has experienced.

2) You will not bring the spirits of past lovers with you to the marriage.

3) You will not have to worry about sexually transmitted diseases because your spouse will be a virgin.

1 Thessalonians 4:3-4(KJV) states

(3) For this is the will of God, even your sanctification, that ye should abstain from fornication: (4) That every one of you should know how to possess his vessel in sanctification and honour;

At the beginning of creation, sex was meant for procreation and for a husband and wife to show real love for one another. But after the fall of man and sin stepped in, the enemy has turned what God has meant to be a beautiful and adoring thing between a man and a woman into something that can be immoral and depraved. He causes the natural order of sexual acts to take on sinful lusts and go against the teachings of our Lord and Savior, Jesus Christ. But know that the Word of God says that the bed of marriage is undefiled not the bed of fornication or adultery.

When a teen's body begins to develop, there are certain urges that come along with it. Their bodies can and do develop at an alarmingly faster rate than their minds. They begin to have adult like urges with a childlike mind. It is important that they understand what their bodies are going through. They need to understand that what they feel is natural, but they need to realize also that they need to try to control those urges. They need to know that they can go to God to help them to subdue the urges. God tells us to make our flesh submit. That means in every aspect of our lives. Sexual urges included.

As our children begin to develop physically, we as parents begin to fear the worse. What am I going to do? How will I manage this? Will I be able to talk to my child and be able to get him/her to understand what their body is going through? We sometimes allow that fear to keep us from being the parent that we need to be in that situation and our children are left to get information from other places. More times than not, they get the incorrect information. So, put that fear on the back burner and parent your child/children even when it is something difficult.

When we look at statistics today, teen pregnancy and sexually transmitted diseases are enough to make us as parents talk to our children continually.

Shaping them into productive parents equipped to take on whatever this world throws their way. Parents, God has set a standard for each of us, and we must do the same for our children. Just as God, the Father, holds us accountable, we must do the same thing for our children. Accountability is high up on the list of standards. Integrity and a good moral fiber are others. Looking to God to help keep us in these things and to help us make the right decisions is the best thing that we can do for our children.

The first thing that we can do is to give them what the Word of God says about it. But remember, if you have not already been teaching about God, using His Word can prove fruitless. It can make them feel like you are ganging up on them. Therefore, be gentle with them and this topic.

God's Word can cuts like a two-edged sword. We want it to do what it is meant to do, but we do not want it to cause your child to feel alienated. His Word is the best recourse we have but if used incorrectly, it can be turned into something negative. God says in loving kindness have I drawn thee. We must draw our children the same way. We must give them the love and attention that it requires to draw them out of the darkness of this world and into the light of Jesus Christ our Savior.

Sex can be a beautiful thing when experienced between a mature man and woman. Those who know what it is to really be in love with someone and not just in lust with them. Love lasts forever and lust is forever fleeting. Teach at an early age what the Word of God is and speaks. It says for you to train a child up in the way that he/she should go and when they are old, they will not depart from it. They may stray, but they will not leave it. Always keep the lines of communication open. That is the only way you will be able to get to them and help them navigate life's choppy waters.

Teach your children that temptations will come from the enemy. He will not leave them alone just because of their age. The younger they are, the harder he will try to make them fall because he does not want them to be with God. Rest assured that the Word of God says in 1 Corinthians 10:13 that there hath no temptation taken you but what is common to man: but GOD is faithful.........but with the temptation also make a way to escape, that ye may be able to bear it. So, no matter the temptation, God makes a way for you to resist the enemy.

Know that there is nothing new under the sun. This means that whatever temptations we endure, Christ endured them as well and much more than we could possibly imagine. That is why He gives us strength to go through our trials and tribulations. He gives us the strength to withstand the storms that arise in our lifetime. We just need to stick close to God and He will cover us with His wings of protection.

Make no mistake about it, just because we are in Christ, that does not mean that we will not have to go through anything. Being a follower of Christ does not make us exempt to trouble. It just means that when we follow Him, we can cast all of our cares upon Him, and He will come to our rescue. He will never leave us nor forsake us. Also, once He has us in the hollow of His hand, no one or nothing will ever be able to take us out.

Some of us as parents, feel that if we teach our children about premarital sex, we would be opening up a door for them to inter in. Know that if you do not teach them, they will learn on their own. Which could lead to false information and misunderstandings about the beauty of sex and waiting for the marriage bed.

I know that in these days, the norm seems to be getting pregnant and then getting married. But I can assure that is not the natural order of the way God wants or intended it to be. He wants us to follow His order. Marriage first and sex is to come after. Parents, guide your children in the ways of righteousness. Teach them to follow God's lead and keep themselves until marriage.

It is not always easy to guide our children in the ways of righteousness, but someone had to do it for us, so we have to do it for them. It was not any different for us. It was not easy for our parents with us, and it will not be easy for us with our children, but it must be done.

Listen to your children. Sometimes they may say things that we are not ready or equipped to hear but listening is key. Pray about whatever it is that you have been told and seek God for the correct answers and the wisdom on how to guide your children. Believe me, you will not regret it. They are precious. Not only to us but even more to God and He wants us to protect, teach, train, and guide them to show them the right way to go in this lifetime. We may not always understand ourselves how to communicate with them, but if we communicate with God, communication with our children will become a natural thing. Be it the sex talk or any topic that they may need our help with.

NOTES ON PREMARTIAL SEX

_____

_____

_____

_____

_____

_____

_____

_____

_____

_____

_____

_____

_____

_____

_____

_____

_____

_____

_____

_____

_____

_____

_____

_____

_____

_____

Unit 3

Your Teen and Smoking, Drugs, Alcohol.

When I was in high school, I would go to the football and basketball games because I was a cheerleader. Many times, I would see some of my classmates and older friends with cigarettes between their fingers. I would think to myself how cool they looked. But in later years, I learned that it was not cool at all. In fact, I found out that quite the opposite was true. It was to me, disgusting. I hated the smell and more importantly, I hated the taste. Yes, I did try it and I hated it.

My mom was a smoker and my neighbor who we considered a brother would sneak her cigarette butts and try and smoke them. I always choked on the smoke. It was disgusting, but I did not want to look like a wimp, so I pretended that it was good. I was dying on the inside. Finally, after 3 or 4 times, I realized that smoking was not for me. I let it go. I now have (8) children of my own and none of them smoke. I am so proud of them for that.

Their dad smoked from the time that he was sixteen. Then one day in his early 30's he put them down and never picked them up again. God delivered him from the cigarettes, and He will do the same for anyone who finds themselves with this addition. Yes, nicotine is addictive. That's why it's so hard for some people to cut themselves loose from it.

Smoking cigarettes may seem cool and harmless but it is (1) against God's teachings (1 Cor. 6;12; Romans 12:2; PS. 119:37); (2) it is addictive; (3) it is harmful to the smoker and the non-smoker alike. In fact, statistics show that second-hand smoke is more dangerous than picking up the cigarette and smoking yourself; (4) tobacco stains your teeth and does not have a pleasant smell.

Be careful with how you handle presenting not smoking to your children. I have found that with anyone, the more you press them not to do something, the more they want to do it. You can call it the 'forbidden fruit syndrome.' We as humans always seem to want what we should not have. Those things that are the worst for us. Cigarettes are just one of the forbidden fruits.

Some would argue that the Bible does not say that smoking goes against God's teaching. The Bible does not specifically say: "Thou shall not smoke." However, it does teach us that our bodies are temples and that belong to the Lord. Therefore, anything that is not edifying to God should not be put in our bodies.

We as parents must come to the realization that although they are children at the time, we are not raising children. We are raising future adults. A lot of parents make that mistake because we forget to prepare our children for the world. We forget that they will have to survive in a world where not everyone marches to the beat of their drum; meaning that we, as Christians must follow God. We must yield and obey his every command.

Smoking is just one of the many vices present in this world today. Drugs and alcohol have become a pandemic today. Not only have they taken control in the lives of many men and women, but they have also trickled down into the lives of many children; boys and girls alike.

Babies are being born with fetal alcohol syndrome because their mothers drank while pregnant. They are also being born prematurely and addicted to drugs having to go through withdrawals. Smoking while pregnant can cause premature and low birth weight. Some mothers are condemning their children to a life of hardship before they are even born.

Parents must take a firm stand when it comes to educating our children about the dangers of smoking, drinking, and using drugs. Again, we must not demand that they do not do it. There are forces out there that are trying to persuade them to try it. Therefore, if you command them not to do it, it then becomes a part of the forbidden fruits. Just like the serpent that tricked Eve in the Garden of Eden, he will speak to your children and try to convince them to disobey you like Adam and Eve disobeyed God.

So instead of the famous one-liner: 'Because I said so, ' it would be best to give them sound Biblical teachings that support what you are saying. You must teach them how not to yield to the temptations of these voices. There are other ways to do this, but the best way is to lead by example. Children tend to emulate what they see. Their way of thinking is that if mommy and/or daddy can do it, then why shouldn't they? We know that this is from the enemy because children are not capable of making grown-up decisions because their minds are not fully developed yet. So as parents, be good examples for your children. Christ and others led by example and the Bible is full of these examples.

There are however cases where the children of drug or alcohol dependent parents become the exception instead of the rule. They make up in their own minds that they will not become a part of statistics and overcome what the world deems as right.

I will use my own children for example. As I stated earlier, my husband and I are the parents of (8) children, the youngest of which is twenty-one. Their father has battled with being addicted to drugs and alcohol for years. He has been in and out of prison because of this. Today, I am eternally grateful to God because He has delivered my husband from his addictions. Also, thanks be to God (Who deserves all the praise), none of our children are drinking, smoking, or using drugs. I give God the glory because He has kept them. It is God that gave them the mindset to follow Him, and it is each of them that have accepted the charge to do so. We did take them to church so that they could learn about God: who He is to them and for them. We studied the Word together and we learned together.

Remember, in all this, communication is the key. Parents, one of the worse things that we can do is to turn a deaf ear on our children when they want to speak out. The topics that they have may be hard for us to hear, but it is in the best interest of our children that we are willing to listen to them and help them work through everything that they are going through.

Set aside a special time for you to be able to

converse with them and then hear what they are saying to you. Do not be judgmental. James 1:19-20 reads: "Wherefore, my beloved brethren, let every man be swift to hear, slow to speak, slow to wrath: for the wrath of man worketh not the righteousness of God.

This is saying as all evil comes from man and all good comes from God, Christians should rely on the Holy Spirit to help us to be balanced. We should listen more than we speak, caring more for our effect upon others. We should not be quick to become angry or enraged when we don't get our own selfish desires." For our anger will not produce the righteousness of God. It will only produce more anger. Even with our children. They may never express it to us openly (sometimes they do), but it will manifest itself in other ways. The enemy will see to that.

Drugs, alcohol, and smoking are detrimental to our

health and the health of our children. Educate them.
The Word of God makes it plain: Train up a child in
the way in which they should go." They are depending
on you.

As parents we must not expect to be able to do
things that are not suitable in front of our children and
then expect them to do the opposite. We can't or
shouldn't live by that old saying: "Do as I say. Not as I
do." That just does not work with all of our children.
Bringing up children is definitely not one size fits all.

There are some children that you as a parent can
just look at and they will get the gist and then there
are those children that you practically have to break
their necks (so to speak) to get them to listen. There
are different strokes for different folks and the same is
true for our children. We have to figure out what
works best with each one of our children because
they are all individuals. They have their own

personalities and characteristics. They learn differently and they react differently to the situations that arise in their lives. Learn your children. Learn their likes and dislikes. Keep an eye on them and pay close attention to them. Know who they are hanging with. Know the good and the bad influences in their lives. Then it would be easier for you to stay abreast of the situations in their young lives.

Some of the influences in our children's lives are outside influences. We must realize that we are not the only ones that have an impact on them. We must know that the flesh is weak, and it can be persuaded to do things that we would not necessarily want our children to partake in. Smoking, drinking, and doing drugs are just some of the things that this world tries to get our children to indulge in. As parents, we have a duty and a responsibility to show our children that these things are not as pleasing as they may seem.

They may satisfy the flesh but will work against the Spirit every time that they indulge in them.

They are unpleasant habits. Even though they may give pleasure to the flesh at the moment, that pleasure is fleeting. It will not last. The worse thing about them is that they kill the endorphins in our brains that bring natural joy. Therefore, the more you partake in it, the more you will have to partake in them in order to try and duplicate that first high that you got from using, smoking, or drinking. Make sure that your children know all the cons of using these mind-altering substances.

NOTES OF SMOKING, DRUGS, ALCOHOL

Unit 4

Bullying and Suicide Among Teens and Tweens

In today's world, the voice of the enemy has taken over in such a way that he is taking control over our children in many ways. There are children that bully, are being bullied, and are committing suicide. There have been cases where children as young as [3] (10) have taken their own lives. Does bullying have anything to do with it? It could, but studies are showing that bullying is more times than not just the straw that breaks the camel's hump. There is something that is already going on that the enemy has chosen to use as a weapon against the child.

- Research from Washington University in St. Louis is narrowing the gap in psychology's understanding of suicidal thoughts in young people. The findings show that such thoughts begin as early as 9 and 10 years old.

- Death by suicide in children has reached a 30-year high in the United States. During middle and high school, 10% to 15% of kids have thoughts of suicide, according to the Centers for Disease Control and Prevention.

- How early in a child's life do these thoughts begin? New research from Washington University in St, Louis is narrowing the gap in psychology's understanding of suicidal thoughts in young people. The findings show that such thoughts begin as early as 9 and 10 years old.
- The research also found that family conflict and parental monitoring are significant predictors of suicidal thoughts, and the majority of

47

children surveyed had caregivers who either didn't know, or didn't report, the suicidal thoughts of the children they are in charge of.

The child could have low self-esteem because they do not feel that they are as smart as the other children. He/she could be overweight and not feeling their best about him/herself. They could feel that they are not as important to their parents as another sibling (which is not necessarily true), but if that is how the child is feeling, it is real to them.

We, as parents must always be aware of our children and their moods. Pay close attention to them and try your level best to know when their mood changes. Listen to what they are saying, even when they are not talking. I find that unspoken words can be heard more clearly than those verbalized. The adage: "Action speaks louder than words" is true. Our child's actions can tell us more about what is going on with him/her than the words that proceed out of his/her mouth. Pay attention. You will be incredibly happy that you did when your child's life is saved. Watch your child's moods. If you have a child that was outgoing and talkative and suddenly you can barely get two words out of them, chances are, something wrong is going on in their lives. Making sure that you are watching them and assuring them that you are there for them, goes a long way in making your child feel loved and wanted. It could also cut through the sound of the voices that are speaking against them and allowing them to hear the voice of God.

Suicide is the result of someone feeling hopeless. They feel that there is no one that understands what they are going through and that they are all alone. The enemy plays on that. He will speak into the ear gates of those in that state and try to convince them that God does not love them and that He does not care. He tries to convince them that death is the best thing for them. Do you want to know how I know?

Well, I have been there.

At the age of about forty-nine, I found myself in the worst place that I had ever been in in my life. I felt like I was sinking into an abyss of despair. My life was hopeless. I felt worthless and I just did not know where to turn. I am a strong African American woman, and we just do not do the counseling thing. At least that is the lie of the enemy that I accepted for myself.

I, at the time, knew who God was. I attended church. I sang on the choir, but I still found myself in a place of feeling lost. One day, my husband had left for work and the two children that were still at home had gone to school. I was at home alone. I was in my bedroom sitting in my recliner.

In the house where we were living at the time, my bedroom was huge. When you entered in, the bathroom was around the corner to the left. So, from the right side of the room, you could not see it. As I said, I was sitting in my recliner with my back turned to where the bathroom was. I was not in a good way because my health was not at its best. I am an epileptic and I also deal with other health issues.

As I was sitting there, I got this image in my mind. It started with me seeing the medicine cabinet in my bathroom. Now, as I stated earlier, it is impossible to see the bathroom from where I was sitting, but in this image, I had a clear view of it.

I sat there in disbelief. Then, the image turned into sort of a movie. In it, I saw myself getting up from the chair, walking to the bathroom and opening the medicine cabinet. I saw the bottles of pills in it. The image was so clear that I could read the labels on the bottles. Then I heard a voice, just as plain as if someone were standing there with me. It spoke and told me that it is as easy as taking the pills, lying down, and going to sleep. This voice began to get louder and louder. It became increasingly convincing. There I was, at the age of forty-nine contemplating suicide. With the entire thing being played out in my mind, I felt it could be easy. Just as I was about to succumb, my telephone rang and on the other end of the phone was my sister, Elaine saying that she needed me. I came back to reality.

After I got off the phone with her, the thoughts came pouring in. If you had done that, it would have been your little girls that would have found you. I immediately thanked God for His mercy because he provided me with a way of escape. My sister calling showed me that I was needed. It showed me that I was not just here for myself but for the benefit of others.

I gave my testimony in this because this is just how the enemy works. He uses these tactics even with our children. He tries to convince them that they are not worthy to be loved. They are not worthy of living. He tries to convince them that the problems that their parents are having are their fault. He makes them believe that they deserve to be bullied and their only way out is death.

Parents, give your children a solid foundation. That foundation is the knowledge of who God is. Knowing and believing in Christ will help them stifle the voice of the enemy. God's voice will lead them away from the dark. He will lead them into the light.

Proverbs 22:6 reads: Train up a child in the way he should go: and when he is old, he will not depart from it.

We must teach our children just who our Lord and Savior, Jesus Christ is and they will have something to give them the strength that they need to endure. It is not always easy to know what to do when dealing with your child, but if you look to God for your own guidance, He will show you the way.

Making sure that your child knows who God is will

lessen the chance of them yielding to the enemy's voice. If you pay close attention to them, it will let them know that they are not alone. They will know that they are loved, and they have a place to go to seek help and that they have hope. Do not allow the hustle and bustle in your own life drown out the voice of your child clearly crying out for help. Take the time to speak with your child/children about suicide. They will listen. More importantly is the fact that they will know that you are interested in being there for them, no matter what.

Be sure that in your caring that you are not becoming overbearing. Sometimes we alienate our children by smothering them. There must be a balance between you caring and you allowing them to be their own person. Make sure that you do not take their voice away. Love them, of course, but do not make them feel like you do not trust them. This could push them in the wrong direction as well. This also goes for the child doing the bullying.

Bullying is another topic that needs to be discussed with your children. Whether they are being bullied or are the one doing the bullying, this is something that they need to be aware of. One thing we as parents must know is that there is always a reason for everything. For the bully, normally there is something going on with them that causes them to want to hurt someone else.

Bullying is about preying on the weak. It is about making someone else feel worse about themselves because of how they feel about himself/herself. If we were to check the life of a bully, I believe that more times than not, we will find that they have been the victim of bullying, or something happened to them to cause them to strike out at others. Or they just simply have low self-esteem and feel that they can make themselves feel better by making someone else feel bad.

One of the best pieces of advice that you could ever give your child/children is: "The only time that someone else's opinion of you matters is if you adopt it as your own." When someone else says how they feel about us, it simply is not our problem nor is it our business. The only opinion that counts is God's. Why, may you ask? It is because He created us, and He knows all about us. So, teach your children self-respect. When they respect themselves, that normally demands respect from others.

Our children are precious jewels. Gifts are given to us from God to nurture and to protect. Someone bullying or being bullied should never be accepted. One of the ways that we should be able to ensure that our children are not doing it is by communicating with them about the dangers of bullying another child. You should try to come to the reason that they have chosen to bully someone else and then help them to work through those issues. Even if you must put them in counseling, your child's best interest should always be at the forefront.

Dealing with a child that is being bullied is a necessity. Your child's mood swings or being withdrawn is an indication that there is something going on with them. Whatever it is, you must reassure them that you are there for them and that they can speak with you about it. Bullying hurts and can be deadly. Not paying attention to your child can be worse.

We as parents may not be able to catch everything but if we do not become so busy with our own lives, we will have time to give our children the attention that they need. This could help to prevent any feelings of loneliness or despair. There are no guarantees but having this kind of relationship with your child gives you a better chance of staying abreast of what is going on in their lives. Which gives you a better chance to head off any trouble.

Parents, be aware, be vigilant, be sympathetic to what your child is going through; be it they are the bullies or the bullied. It is never too late if your child is still with you, but there is no time like the present. Trust that when you show your interest, they will respond. Most children just want the attention from their parents. Give it to them. You will not regret it.

Bullying does not only happen with other children in the school, on the playground, or on the internet. It can happen in your own home between siblings. As parents, we must look for the signs that our children are being bullied. Not just by other children, but by their siblings or even sometimes adults. In fact, parents must be very aware to make sure that our parenting does not filter over into bullying. It can and does happen. Many times, children who are bullied by their parents, turn into children who bully (because children learn what they see) and then grow up to be adults who bully. They bully people in the home and even on the job. It is as if a switch has been turned on that they cannot turn off without professional help. So be careful that your parenting is parenting and not bullying.

Be it the one who is bullied or the one doing the bullying, they both need help. When a child is bullied, more times than not, it gives them low self-esteem. The bullies could have low self-esteem as well. They could be in a place that they feel that if they did not do it to someone else, it would be done to them. Most times, they are more afraid than the person that they are bullying. If you were to speak with someone that used to be a bully, they would probably tell you that these things are true.

When I was a little girl, we called it being picked on. I was a small child and because of this, I was picked on a great deal. It was never just one person. It was a group of girls that picked on me. So not much has changed since the '60s and '70s concerning this except the name and the ways by which it can be done, because more times than not, it is a group that bullies a child.

One of the biggest warning signs is a change in their personality or demeanor. If your child was at one point outgoing and lively and then she/he becomes withdrawn, that is a sign that there is something going on. Although there could be other causes, bullying could be at the core. Again, I say, pay attention to your child/children. Do not be that parent that has no time for them. Do not be that parent who allows things to parent your children.

No, parents are not perfect and there will be times that we miss the signs. But, if we have developed a sound relationship with our children, the chances of that happening will lessen. Sometimes you will get on their nerves by staying in their faces especially when you see a change in them. Truthfully, it is in the child's best interest to do this. They will appreciate it when they are older. Just as we did not like many of the parenting decisions that our parents made when we were young, after we had our own children, we found ourselves making some of those same decisions. We came to know that they were the best things for us even though we did not think so at the time.

As a working mother of (8), I was not able to catch everything that my own children went through. I regret that to this day. But I am eternally grateful to God that He kept them in the things that they had to endure. This is one of the reasons for my writing this book. I want to try to impact the lives of parents and help you all to manage the issues in your children's lives.

Please, listen to your children and be attentive to them. When they know that they have a safe haven in you, they will be more susceptible to opening up to you. Being the voice of reason for them will block the hand of the enemy. Giving them what they need spiritually, emotionally, and physically puts them in a place of peace and joy and makes their lives less stressful.

NOTES ON BULLYING

_____

_____

_____

_____

_____

_____

_____

_____

_____

_____

_____

_____

_____

_____

_____

_____

_____

_____

_____

_____

_____

_____

_____

NOTES ON SUICIDE

Unit 5

Homosexuality: DNA or Choice?

Homosexuality is a topic that is avoided by many. It is, however, something that we do need to discuss with our children. It is very controversial. There are those who say that it is as natural as being a heterosexual and that they are born that way. Then there are those who go by what the Word of God says concerning it. So, for this segment, to avoid giving you my feelings, opinions, or beliefs, I will give you what God's Word says.

First, I will say to you that we are never to look down on someone for their sexual orientation. While we should not condone the act, we cannot alienate our children either. The Word of God says to love the sinner but hate the sin. That is what we must do for our children. We must love them no matter what so that we will not risk losing them in a world of sin.

For any parent, it can be devastating to hear that their child is gay, but if you are equipped with the Word of God, you will be capable of dealing with it without causing a rift between you and your child. Knowing the Word can and will help you to manage the situation with love while still praying for your child's deliverance.

Know that we need deliverance from all manner of sin. This is not the only sin that God frowns upon. He is the only Wise God and He and He alone can deliver all of us from death.

1 Corinthians 15:55-57 (KJV)

- O death, where is thy sting? O grave, where is thy victory?
- The sting of death is sin; and the strength of sin is the law.
- But thanks be to God, which gives us the victory through Jesus Christ.

As I stated earlier, I will only be giving you what the Word of God is concerning this. Know that God frowns upon all sin, but He says Himself that this is an abomination.

I am fully aware of the studies that they have out there now concerning same-sex activity. They say that there is now proof that there is a gene that makes someone gay. I find it extremely hard to believe because the Word of God teaches against it. With that being said, we do not serve a God who would make someone that way and then condemn them for being said way. That would be like Him condemning me for being an African American woman. I had no choice in what nationality or gender I was born. So, God simply would not do such a thing because He is a loving God. Make sure that your child knows that God loves them no matter what. He just wants them to choose life instead of death.

Proverbs 14:12 says that there is a way that seems right to a man, but the end thereof leads to death. Homosexuality is just one of those ways. Believing that because of God's grace you have a license to sin is another.

God's grace and mercy are there for us, but they are not there for us to live any way we want to. God wants us to obey His Word and follow in the footsteps of Christ. Choosing to follow God is the best thing that any person can do. Choosing God and making Him first in your life will help you to come out of and stay out of sin. It does not matter what it is; homosexuality included.

Just because a person is a heterosexual, that does not mean that we are free from sin. We must abide by God's commands just as anyone else. We had to surrender to God to be brought up out of sin just like anyone else. Romans 3:23 says for all have sinned and come short of the glory of God. That means each and every one of us. It is just that those who are now in Christ made the choice to give our lives to Him.

I know for some parents this could be one of the

last things that they would want to hear their children say to them. But you must continue to love them no matter what. Loving them does not mean that you must compromise with the sin. Again, God says to hate the sin but love the sinner. To do this, you must look to God for the strength, wisdom, knowledge, and understanding on how to do it.

As I stated earlier, I am only going to give what the Word of God says about this topic and not my opinion. Here are a few Scriptures to show what God says.

Leviticus 18:22

This Scripture specifically tells us that a man should not lie with a man as he lies with a woman. It calls it an abomination. An abomination is the English term used to translate the Biblical Hebrew term 'shiqquts.' It is that which is exceptionally loathsome, hateful, sinful, wicked, or vile.

Leviticus 20:13

Here we see again that the Scripture is speaking a man lying with a man as he would a woman. It says that they both have committed and abomination. It further says that they will be put to death. For those that would argue that these are Old Testament views, I will provide you with what the New Testament has to say about it as well.

Romans 1:18-32

These passages of Scripture are speaking explicitly to those that gave up the truth of God and yield to other gods. They gave themselves over to all ungodliness. They did so much so that God turned them over to a reprobate mind which means that because of their disobedience, they will think that that which is wrong is right. It even speaks about the women turning to unnatural acts with women.

Here are some other Scriptures that teach against

it:

1 Corinthians 6:9-11

1 Timothy 10

The sin of same-sex activity is not the only sin that the Bible speaks of, but it is called an abomination because it is a sin committed against your own body. 1 Corinthians 1:19 states that the body is the temple of the Holy Ghost which is in us. It also lets us know that we do not belong to ourselves but to God who created us.

Genesis 1:20-24 tells us what God intended marriage to be. It is for a man and a woman and not (2) men or (2) women. 1 Corinthians 7:2 says that a man should have his own wife and a woman her own husband.

God is specific on this, but because of Who He is, you can repent and seek His forgiveness. He is just and able to deliver you out of your sin no matter what it is. He wants all of us to turn around and come to Him. God is a Merciful God. His Grace and Mercy are here to keep us but they in no wise give us a license to sin. They are there to cover us when we sin, but we must not be willfully sinning. We cannot continue to walk in sin and expect to be covered. When you know that you are doing wrong, God expects us to do better.

If you find yourself in the position where your child has been deceived into thinking that he/she is trapped in the wrong body, do not allow the lies of the enemy to prevail. Continue to love on your child and pray for them. The love of God will prevail. You just cannot give up. Jesus' love covers a multitude of sin. We must teach our children that they can trust in and rely on Jesus to be there. Help them to study His Word. The closer they get to God, the louder His voice will become, and it will stifle the voice of the enemy.

Remember to love your child unconditionally. Do not compromise with the sin but reassure your child that they have your love. Think about how God loved

us out of our sin, and He will do the same thing for our

children.

NOTES ON HOMOSEXUALITY

Unit 6

Teaching About God

This Unit is near and dear to my heart for it will be discussing our Heavenly Father and how to instruct your children about Him. I in no wise am saying that any of my readers have not already been educating their children about Christ and His love for His children.

As stated before, the Word of God tells us in Proverbs 22:6, "Train up a child in the way he should go: and when he is old, he will not depart from it." (KJV)

The Word does not say that they will not stray. It simply says that they will not depart from it. For I am quite sure that many of my readers and others as well, were taught as children about God, but when we grew up, many strayed from that teaching (yours truly included) because we wanted to do our own thing.

But as time went by, we came to our senses and returned to our first love.

In 1 Corinthians 13:11 Paul said: "When I was a child, I spoke as a child, I understood as a child, I thought as a child: but when I became a man, I put away childish things." For me, this means that before he knew who God is, he did childish things. Those childish things that he did were his persecution of the church of God. He captured Christians, threw them in jail and even murdered many. But he met God on the road to Damascus, his childish things were put away. He became the greatest of the Apostles. So much so that he authored more books of the entire Bible than any other author.

But isn't it ironic that Paul, being a persecutor of Christians, suffered many of the same things that he did to them by his hand? He was imprisoned. He was hunted by those who sought to do him harm. He was also murdered just like those Christians that he murdered.

Even though he reconsidered and served God well, he still had to suffer the consequences of his actions. My point being you reap what you sew. God will forgive us for our actions but that does not mean that we will not have to pay for what we did. Not with our lives, because Jesus atoned for our sins. But we will be chastised for our deeds. God says that He chastens those whom He loves.

It is just like us with our very own children. When they disobey us, we still love them, but we punish them to teach them not to be disobedient. That is what God does for us. He does not want any of us to be lost so He will chastise us.

However, just like us, Paul's suffering was not in vain. God entrusted him with His Word. He even wrote the Prison Epistles which he penned while he was in prison. These include Philippians, Ephesians, Colossians, and Philemon.

Parents, teach your children that when we are living sinful lives, we are very much so being childish. But when we come into the knowledge of Christ, we can put away our sins. Thus, putting away those childish things that can cause a separation between us and God. Christ died to redeem us from the hand of the enemy. His death reconciled us to God. He is the substitutionary sacrifice for our sins. He paid the price so that we would not have to pay it for ourselves. Besides, we could not pay for it anyway.

To get to heaven, we must accept Christ as our Lord and Savior and follow God's commands by obeying the Holy Spirit. Know that Heaven is a prepared place for a prepared people. That is why

God sent His only begotten Son to prepare His people for His second coming.

John 3:16

- For God so loved the world, that He gave His only begotten Son, that whosoever believeth in Him should not perish, but have everlasting life.

God loves His people just that much. He did not withhold His own Son from death. We, as parents must make sure that they know that there is a much better life than what this world has to offer. Christ said that He came to give life and to give it more abundantly. He is our Lord and Savior, our Bridge over troubled waters, our Strong Tower, our Lily in the valley, our Provider, Protector, and our Inspiration.

So, show your children how to respect God for Who He is. Teach them how to go to God for themselves. Teach them how to love and respect each other. For the Word says that we cannot love Him whom we have never seen and not love our brother whom we see every day. God is Love and we too must show love.

We must live our lives so that we can live again. We may not see a physical death, but we must be ever so vigilant so that we will not suffer a spiritual death. We must apply the Word to our lives and teach our children to do the same. It is easy. Just put your hands in God's hands and be led by the Holy Spirit.

Instruct your children about God because He has a special anointing on them and a special calling for them.

Jeremiah 1:5 (KJV)
- Before I formed them in the belly I k new thee: and before thou camest forth out of the womb I sanctified thee, and I ordained thee a prophet unto the nations.

Psalm 139:13-18
- For thou hast possessed my reins: thou hast covered me in my mother's womb.
- I will praise thee; for I am fearfully and wonderfully made: marvelous are thy works; and that my soul knoweth right well.
- My substance was not hid from thee, when I was made in secret, and curiously wrought in the lowest parts of the earth.
- Thine eyes did see my substance, yet being unperfect; and in Thy book all my members were written, which in continuance were fashioned, when as yet there was none of them.
- How precious also are Thy thoughts unto me, O God! How great is the sum of them!
- If I should count them, they are more in number than the sand: when I awake, I am still with thee.

These are the perfect passages to show your children who they are in Christ and in God. When we look at God's workmanship, we can see the beauty that it is and that we are fearfully and wonderfully made. The intricate details with which He has designed every one of us could only be wrought by God's hands. He gave us the ability to think and make rational choices. Yet we still cannot fathom the power of the mind.

If we were to try to study the workings and design of our minds, it would take about one hundred lifetimes and we still will barely touch the surface. That is just how great our God is. Our little finite minds cannot begin to comprehend all of His works. Yet, when we go to Him in fasting and prayer, He will reveal things about His Word and His works to us. But know that He will only reveal that which we can handle. Remember, His Word says that He will not put more on us than we can bear. That does not only go for the bad. It goes for the good as well.

Knowing God is not just believing that He exists
or quoting Scriptures. The Word says in James 2:19 that thou believeth that there is one God: thou doest well. The devils also believe—and tremble. Therefore, we must trust, obey His commands, and have faith in Him. That is what a true relationship with God is all about. 2 Timothy 2:15 says to study to shew thyself approved unto God, a workman that needeth not to be ashamed, rightly dividing the Word of Truth.

Studying God's Word will enable you to get to Him for whom He really is. He is our Lord and our Savior primarily. Then He is our Provider, Protector, Healer, Comforter, Peace, Joy, and Confidante. He is so many things to us and for us and also through us.

Having a relationship with Christ is the best decision that anyone can make. Especially for parents. Not only for you as a parent but for your children as well. When they see you carrying the characteristics of Christ and living it in your daily lives, they will follow in your footsteps. Even if they stray, they will not depart from it. The voice of God (which some call a conscious) will be the voice of reason for them.

Having a relationship with God is being able to communicate with Him. Communication with God is simply praying to Him.

What is Prayer?

- It is a solemn request for help or expression of thanks and adoration addressed to God.

Philippians 4:6

- Be careful for nothing; but in every thing by prayer and supplication with thanksgiving let your requests be made known unto God.

God wants us to make every request known to Him. Because He cares about what we care about, He wants us to come to Him in prayer rather than worrying about anything.

Make no mistake about it, God already knows what you need and what you want. But He wants you to come to Him because in doing so, that lets Him know that you trust Him and believe in His power and in His might.

Know that God loves us unconditionally and He always wants the best for each of us. But the thing we must realize is that God always answers our prayers. His answers come in the form of a yes, no, or wait. Whatever the answer is that He gives, it will be the best for the situation at hand.

Sometimes we feel like God is not hearing us. We may even feel like God has left us, but we must understand that even when we cannot trace Him, we must trust Him. Also, delay does not mean denied. God is just and able to supply all of our needs according to His riches in glory. Trust and believe, God is the Living God, the only Wise God, and His love is from everlasting to everlasting. His mercy endureth forever.

Teach your children how to believe in God. Teach them to trust in God. Teach them how to have faith in God. Those are the greatest lessons that they will ever learn. The Holy Bible is the best teacher that we will ever have. Teach them how to study His Word and how to meditate on It.

Teach your children how to pray. Let them know that prayer is just a conversation with God in which you pour out your most inner thoughts, desires, and adoration for God.

Let your children know that they can speak with God just like they speak to you, their parents. God is always listening to hear the voices of His children. Prayer is the key and faith unlocks the door. We can go to God in prayer and all of our worries and concerns can be poured out to Him. Teach them how to pray properly. In praying, we must learn how to pray God's will.

In Matthew 6, Christ gives an example of the model prayer. In it, there are praises to the Lord God, the expression of our needs, the desire to be forgiven and the need to forgive, and the request for guidance and deliverance. This is the perfect example on how to pray God's will over our lives. God's way is the only way of redemption, restoration, reconciliation, and repentance. These are the four (R's) of righteousness.

It is true that God has given His people free will, but He still wants us to love and to choose Him. It is just like us with our own children; we want to feel loved by them. We want to be respected and not rejected by them. More than anything else, we want it to be genuine and not because they fear us as though we are evil forces in their lives. This is why God gave His children free will. He did not create an army of robots but a people that have the right to choose good (God) or evil (Satan). Teach your children that choosing good over evil is the best choice that they could ever make.

Proverbs 9:10
   The fear of the Lord is the beginning of wisdom: and the knowledge of the Holy is understanding,

This fear that is being spoken of is not one of being afraid but instead, it is one of respect and adoration.

NOTES ON TEACHING ABOUT GOD

Conclusion

In the world today, there are many evils and temptations that will try to draw our children. We, parents, must become world overcomers so that we can keep our children out of the world and in the Kingdom of God. We also must teach them how to become world overcomers. We may not always know the right thing to do or the correct answers for some of the situations that arise, but when we look to God, the Author and Finisher of our Faith, we can get the wisdom and knowledge that we need to guide our children.

Overcomers are followers of Jesus Christ and are able to resist the wiles of the enemy. First John 5:4-5 tells us that whatever is born of God overcomes the world, and this is the victory that overcomes the world----our Faith. Who is the one who overcomes the world, but he who believes that Jesus Christ is the Son of God? Jesus, in the book of Revelation, tells us to be steadfast through our trials and tribulations. That is how we become overcomers.

As previously stated, our children are precious jewels and they deserve to be loved, nurtured, and brought up in the way in which they should go. Teaching them what God says about the way we should live is the best thing that we can do for them. God is our Creator, and we must worship, praise, and glorify Him because He is worthy.

The life that we lead should speak more loudly than the things that we say. Our children do learn what they see. We may think that saying to them do as I say and not as I do will work, but that is just not true for them, or anyone else.

Of course, our children should be obedient to what

we tell them, but let us be honest, they develop their own minds and ways. They develop characteristics of their own but when they see their parents following God's Word, they will be more apt to follow suit. Therefore, it would be best to lead by example.

They are not equipped to manage what they are faced with today, so we, as parents, must be there for them in every situation. We must teach them that things will not always go their way, but if they put their trust in God, it will not matter because it will work out for their good in the end. That is the promise of Romans 8:28.

Parents, we may not always know the perfect thing to do or to say, so we must listen to hear God's voice. Doing so allows His voice to guide us in every situation. It helps us to go forward in life on the right path and teaches us how to put our children on that path as well. So, accept God's Word as It gives wisdom on how to do this.

The world says that its ok for our children to do so many things that the Word of God teaches against. Premarital sex, smoking, drinking, using drugs, bullying, and homosexuality are just a few in a line of sins that are growing in the world. There are countless other issues that they will face on a day-to-day basis. Equipping them with the knowledge of God's Word is the first and best defense against these things.

God speaks against these things, but it is not too late for them to repent and allow God to deliver them out of these sins. He is waiting on them to turn away from sin and turn to Him. He is just and able to forgive them. God loves us and He also created us which means He does not want any of us to be lost. That is just the kind of God that He is. Parents, allow God to lead you on how to lead your children. Becoming a world overcomer is the best and most important thing that you can do for yourself and your child.

The only way to do that is to trust God. Trust in His Word. Trust in His voice. Trust Him to lead and guide you so that you will know how to speak to your children in love and kindness. Remember, God is love and in loving-kindness has He drawn each of His children. So, we must do the same for our own children.

Following God will never be a mistake. It is the best choice anyone could ever make. Make the choice and allow God to build His hedge of protection around you and your children. You will not regret it.

In my conclusion, I will leave you with this: the Word of God is good. It is a life changer. It is also life sustaining. In fact, it is Life Itself. But it will not be effective unless it is applied to our lives and the lives of our children. Read it. Study it. Meditate on it and then apply it. It works.

THE END!

PERSONAL NOTES AND DIARY

This section is for you, as parents, to be able to write down those personal thoughts that you may have. It is also to record the actions of your children so that you will be able to keep track of their different moods and know if there is a major change. Paying close attention to your child will make them feel loved and wanted. It will stop the enemy from being able to convince them that no one cares because they are not worthy of being loved.

Use this section to write down your innermost thoughts and different strategies to help your children deal with all the issues that may come up against them. Also, write down any questions that they may have so that you may search the Scriptures to find the answers to those questions. God's Holy Word has answers to any and every situation that may arise. Use it. It will not fail you. Know that as parents, we may not be able to catch everything. But with diligence, patience, love, and endurance, we will be able to combat the enemy. When he comes up against our children, we must be vigilant and fight for them with every bit of power that we have as children of God. We can never give up or give out. We must not fear.

2 Timothy 1:7
- For God has not given us the spirit of fear; but of power, and of love, and of a sound mind.

Fear is of the devil, and it can only serve its purpose if you allow it to. We must always stand up and stand out even in the face of adversity. We are able to do this if we trust in God and have the faith to know that He will never leave us nor forsake us. That is God's promise of safety to His children. Check Psalms 91.

As you are journaling, always keep in mind those things that you observe your child doing. I am not suggesting that you smother your child because that can alienate them. But watch without them knowing that you are watching. Be ever vigilant and keep a watchful eye on them. Learn their every mood and different emotions. Trust me, your child will be better off for it in the end.

SCRIPTURES TO ENCOURAGE YOUR CHILD TO DEVELOP A

RELATIONSHIP WITH GOD:

Deuteronomy 6:6-7; 11:18-19
- These Scriptures encourage us to talk about God.

Psalm 78:4-7
- This tells us that we ought to make God's law known to our children.

2 Corinthians 5:20
- This tells us how we should be representatives of Christ. Our child watches and learns from what we say and do. Therefore, we must live Godly lives for them.

Matthew 19:13-15
- This teaches us that we must be like children. Teach your children to remain humble.

1 Timothy 4:10-11
- Teach your children that they should have hope in the living God.

Proverbs 3:5-6
- This lets you know to trust the Lord with all your heart and all your mind and to lean not to your own understanding.

Jeremiah 29:11
- God knows the plans that He has for us. So, we must trust Him and know that He won't let us down. The plans that He has for us may not be exactly what we have for ourselves, but we can rest assured that it will work out for our good. That is the Romans 8:28 promise.

Matthew 7:11
- This tells us that we should go to God in prayer. He hears and He will answer. Teach your children to go to God for themselves. Teach them how to pray.

Joshua 1:9
- This is telling us not to fear. Teach your children that when they are in relationship with God, there is no need to fear because He is always with you. Even though some things may happen that you may not like, it won't take you out, it will just make you stronger.

2 Timothy 2:15

- This is telling you to study the Word of God for yourself. You will be able to develop the right relationship with Him. Studying His Word will help you to draw closer to Him.

Explaining the Scriptures

This section is designed to help you and your child/children delve into the Scriptures so that you may get a deeper understanding and revelation of God's Word. Remember to always pray before you undertake the study of the Word. This will help you to be able to hear God's voice as you and your child are studying. Seek Him in everything that you do, say, or think.

Proverbs 3:5-6

- Trust in the Lord with all thine heart; and lean not unto thine own understanding.
- In all thy ways acknowledge Him, and He shall direct thy paths.

Matthew 6:33

- But seek ye first the Kingdom of God, and His righteousness; and all these things shall be added unto you.

These Scriptures, among many others, are telling you to put God first in your lives. In everything we do, everything we say, everything that we think, and whatever we choose to eat or drink. Keep God first and He will direct our paths. Putting us on the straight and narrow and keeping us there. He will keep us in the valley low and on the mountain high. God will be with us in the good times and in the bad times.

God does not want us to only seek Him when things have gone awry in our lives. He wants us to praise Him in the good times as well. He always wants us to put a praise on every situation that arises in our lives: the good, the bad, and the ugly. Give God a praise. When we praise Him, it helps the situations in our lives seem not so scary or impossible.

References:

Bible

- KJV
  Copyright 1995 by Zandervan
  Published by Zandervan
  Grand Rapids, Michigan 49530 USA
Melendez Brothers
- Zarakin, Jordan
  July 20, 2020
Suicide Among Teens and Tweens
- Jefferson, Brandie
  THE SOURCE
  February 7, 2020
- Barch, Deanna
  - Chair and Professor of Psychological and Brain Sciences
    In Arts & Sciences and Professor of Radiology in the School
    Of Medicine.
  - University of St. Louis
    St. Louis, MO

ABOUT THE ARTHOR

I am a 62-year-old wife of 44 years to my husband, Christopher; mother of eight; grandmother of seventeen; and great-grandmother of seven. I was born and raised in a small town in Berkeley County in South Carolina. I was educated in the school system there. I am number nine out of ten children of my parents, John and Beatrice Dingle. They were both Christians and they instructed my brothers and sisters and I to love and obey God. I accepted Christ at an early age, and I was baptized at the age of twelve at the Day Dawn Baptist Church in Pineville, SC. I began writing during my high school years; mostly poetry and plays.

My life has been a series of hills and valleys but because of the love of my Lord and Savior, Jesus Christ, I made it through, and I am still standing.

At the age of fifty, I was diagnosed with Myelofibrosis, which is a chronic form of Leukemia. But praise be to my God, I am healed. I was also an epileptic and God has also delivered me from the seizures as well.

I am giving a portion of my testimony to let you, my readers, know that God is just and able to do just what you need Him to do. He is no respecter of persons. So, since He did it for me, He will do it for you as well.

I am also a published author. My first work is entitled: "As the Storm Goes Passing By." It is a book of poetry that I wrote over the years.

I am an elder in my ministry, Kingdom-Minded Ambassadors Deliverance Ministries where the Apostle Pernell Applewhite, Jr. is the Overseer alongside of Elder Kenya Applewhite, his wife, who is the Pastor. The ministry was established in 2011 in St. Stephen, SC and later moved to Timmonsville, SC.
It is because of God that I was able to author this book to help my readers get through some of the difficult times while raising their teens. Being a mother myself, I know how difficult it can be. So, we need all the encouragement that we can get. Remember the old African adage: "It takes a village to raise a child." Let us all be a part of that village. God bless you.